THE FOTOFLITE FI

Volume 1: Royal Navy Wars

Steve Bush

OFC
Built by Vospers at Portchester and launched in January 1958. She was accepted in January 1960 where she joined the Coastal Forces Trials Unit attached to HMS DOLPHIN. In August 1962 she joined the Fishery Protection Squadron before decommissioning in April 1970 to be laid up at Hythe. In 1972 she was placed in reserve at Portsmouth prior to service as a target at Pembroke Dock. (*Image No: BWA192*)

Frontispiece
HM Ships BLEASDALE (foreground) and OPPORTUNE. A Type III Hunt class destroyer, BLEASDALE was built by Vickers Armstrong and completed in April 1942. In August that year she took part in the Dieppe raid and escorted Channel and North Sea convoys. In April 1943 she sank U-203. Post-war she was recalssified as a frigate and was used as a target ship prior to being placed in reserve in 1952. She was broken up at Blyth in 1956. OPPORTUNE was an Emergency War class destroyer built by John Thornycroft, Woolston, and commissioned on 14 August 1942. She served throughout WWII, mainly as an escort ship for convoys, though she took part in the Battle of North Cape and the destruction of the SCHARNHORST. Post-war she operated from Portsmouth for submarine training and Local Flotilla duties until 1950. She then refitted and joined the Nore Local Flotilla. She entered reserve at Chatham in 1952 before being moved to Portsmouth the following year. On 25 November 1955 she was towed to Milford Haven to be broken-up by Thos. W. Ward. (*Image No: BW5946*)

First published in the United Kingdom in 2017 by NavyBooks, Unit 6B, Heathlands, Liskeard, Cornwall, PL14 4DH

INTRODUCTION

The photographs used throughout this book are taken from the Fotoflite collection. Fotoflite have been photographing the World's shipping since the 1950s, and have a photo archive of over 1/2 million aerial maritime photographs. The collection is well known throughout the world, but while most associate it with merchant shipping, there is a vast collection of warship images dating back to the 1950s. Weather permitting, Fotoflite fly the length and breadth of the English Channel, capturing the widest range of shipping in one of the world's busiest shipping lanes.

This volume, the first in a series, has gathered together dozens of black & white images of Royal Navy, Royal Fleet Auxiliary, Army and Port Service vessels recorded since the 1950s. It is a fascinating insight into a period of transition from the end of a global conflict, through the Cold War and into the nuclear age.

Copies of photographs used in this book may be obtained from Fotoflite direct quoting the image number displayed below each entry.

Their website, www.fotoflite.com, lists over 460,000 aerial maritime photos, and over 377,888 have been digitised and can be viewed on the site. They are continually adding new photographs, and working through digitising their archive, so the number is growing all the time.

To order copies visit the website or e-mail: jon@fotoflite.co.uk

If you are not online write to: Fotoflite, 10 Stafford Close, Ashford, Kent, TN23 4TT, UK or phone +44 (0) 1233 635556

HMS ACUTE, an Algerine class minesweeper was built by Harland and Wolff at Belfast. She was launched on 14 April 1942 and completed on 30 July the same year. She operated in the Mediterranean earning the battle honours North Africa 1942-43, Sicily 1943 and Salerno 1943. She returned to the UK in 1946 and in November paid off into reserve at Harwich. in 1956 she was refitted and commissioned for service with the Dartmouth Training Squadron. She paid off in 1961 and was sold at Malta in 1964 after use as a torpedo target and broken up at La Spezia.

HMS ACUTE (Image No: BWX7176)

An 'A' class submarine built by Cammell Laird, Birkenhead, and commissioned on 31 July 1946. The 'A' class were designed during WWII for service in the Pacific, where the distances involved required a submarine with a higher surface speed and greater endurance. Habitability was also improved through the introduction of air conditioning. Completed too late to see service in WWII the submarines were gradually modernised through the mid to late 1950s, streamlining the casings to make them faster and less noisy. AENEAS was loaned to Vickers Shipbuilding Group from July to November 1972 to be fitted with SLAM (Submarine Launched Air Missile) in order to carry out test and demonstration firings. Although the trials were successful the system was not pursued as it had too short a range. Replaced by the more modern Porpoise and Oberon classes AENEAS was broken up by Clayton & Davie Ltd, Dunston, from December 1974.

HMS AENEAS (Image No: BW20403)

A Later Battle class destroyer she was built by Hawthorn Leslie and completed on 25 June 1957. The design of these vessels was heavily influenced by war experience and the need for destroyers capable of operations in the Pacific. They carried a heavy AA armament but they were criticised in some circles for having their all of the main armament concentrated forward - some even concluding that ships of such size should have more turrets aft. From 1959-62 she was converted to a Fleet Radar Picket, as seen here, with the addition of a large lattice mast forward to support the Type 965 air warning radar. Larger deck-houses aft supported a second mast with a height-finding radar. The ships were to operate ahead of the main fleet to provide advance warning of approaching aircraft. She was also equipped with a Seacat missile launcher aft. She was reduced to Operational Reserve in 1966 and placed on the disposal list in 1972. She was broken up in Sunderland in 1974.

HMS AGINCOURT (Image No: BWH290)

Built by Cammell Laird, Birkenhead, she was originally laid down as the Type 12 frigate FOWEY, but completed as a Leander class frigate in 1964. She initially served with the 24 EG in the Far East and in 1970 operated as the Gibraltar guardship. In 1970 she entered refit at Devonport, emerging in 1973 as an Ikara conversion, her twin 4.5-inch turret being replaced by an Ikara ASW missile launcher. During the conversion the two 40mm guns were repositioned from the hangar roof to aft of the bridge wings and two quad Seacat launchers mounted in their place. She paid off in 1985, becoming a harbour training ship at Devonport. In 1988 she arrived at Millom, Cumbria, for breaking up.

A Centaur class light fleet carrier built by Swan Hunter on the Tyne. She was launched on 6 May 1947 and completed in 1954. She took part in the Suez campaign in 1956 and served in the Far East and Southern Oceans until 1960. She was converted to a Commando carrier at Portsmouth from 1961-62 and after trials, once again, left for the Far East. She was involved in the Malayan and Indonesian border dispute of 1963. In 1967 she assisted in the withdrawal from Aden. Her final commission took her to the Arctic and Far East before being laid up in 1972. She was sold in 1973 and broken up at Faslane.

One of the numerically large Ham class of post war minesweeper ALTHAM was designed for inshore minesweeping operations. She was built by Camper & Nicholson and completed in July 1953. Most were armed with a 20mm Oerlikon forward, but some, as here, carried the larger 40mm Bofors. ALTHAM was attached to the 232nd MSS at Harwich before entering reserve, at Rosneath, in 1957. Two years later she was transferred to Malaysia as KD SRI JOHOR. She was broken up in 1967.

HMS ALVERTON was one of a class of 119 Ton class coastal minesweepers completed. She was built by Camper & Nicholson and completed in March 1954. Diesel powered vessels of 440 tons displacement fully laden, the Ton class were largely constructed from aluminium and other non-ferromagnetic materials. The hull was composed of a double layer of mahogany planking. ALVERTON was assigned to the London Division Royal Naval Reserve from 1954-62 where she served as HMS THAMES. Following service in the Far East she was towed from Singapore in 1967 and laid up at Gibraltar. From there she was sold to the Irish Naval Service in 1971 becoming LÉ BANBA. In 1984 she was decommissioned and sold for breaking up in Spain.

An 'A' class submarine built by Vickers Armstrong, Barrow, and commissioned on 18 November 1947. She is seen here in her 'as built' configuration, mounting a 4-inch gun. The submarine sustained damage forward on 3 October 1960, when she struck an uncharted rock at 110ft in the Hauraki Gulf, off North Island, New Zealand. The submarine was able to surface safely and reach port under her own power - however, her name lives on as the rock is now charted as Anchorite Rock. The submarine was sold in 1970 and she arrived to be broken up at Troon in August of that year.

A further 'A' class submarine HMS ANDREW was built by Vickers Armstrong, Barrow, and completed in 1948. She was the first submarine to cross the Atlantic submerged using the 'snort' in May 1953. The 2,500-nautical mile trip was made from Bermuda to England and took 15 days in total. It set a new world record for continuous underwater operation. She was also the last in the class to have a 4-inch deck gun fitted - it was mounted in 1964 for service during the Indonesia-Malaysia confrontation to counter blockade running junks. She was sold to be broken up for scrap on 5 May 1977, the work being conducted by Davis and Cann Ltd at Plymouth.

A Leander class frigate, she was built by J.S. White of Cowes and completed in 1965. She was one of the first to receive the Seacat missile system from build. In the later part of the 1960s she operated in the Mediterranean and West Indies. In 1970 she deployed to the Far East, taking part in the Beira Patrol en route. She took part in the Second Cod War, colliding with the ICGV ODINN on 10 August 1973. She emerged from an Ikara conversion in 1977. In 1985 she was fitted with towed array sonar (removed from LOWESTOFT), mounted centrally on the quarterdeck. The VDS well was plated in and the Limbo removed and the well plated over to accommodate the sound room. The ship was decommissioned in 1985 and sunk as a target in 1991.

HMS ARETHUSA (Image No: BW684529)

An 'A' class submarine, she built by Scotts Shipbuilding & Engineering Co., Greenock, and completed in 1947. In July 1971 she sank in 9 metres of water while moored at HMS Dolphin during refuelling. The boat sank by the stern when water rushed into open hatches which couldn't be closed as cables and hoses were connected through them. She was raised on 6 July and de-commissioned. She was sold to be broken up for scrap at Pounds, Portsmouth, in December 1971.

HMS ARTEMIS (Image No: BWX666)

One of 30 LCT (8) landing craft completed for the Royal Navy before the end of WWII. Post war the ships were given names and nine went on to serve during the Suez crisis. This highlighted the Army's need to train landing craft crews and consequently, in 1957, 12 vessels were transferred to the Army and based at Portsmouth. All were given names beginning with the letter 'A' and initially were designated as Royal Army Service Corps Vessels (RASCV). With the amalgamation of the RASC and the transportation arm of the Corps of Royal Engineers in 1965, the Royal Corps of Transport was formed and it was decreed that all RCT vessels would have their prefix changed to Her Majesty's Army Vessel. AUDEMER was converted to a squadron HQ ship in 1961 and thus had an enlarged superstructure to house HQ staff.

HMAV AUDEMER (Image No: BWA260)

An 'A' class submarine, she was built by Vickers Armstrong, Barrow, and completed on 7 February 1947. She took part in the Coronation Fleet Review in 1953 and in 1958 was deployed to the Indian Ocean for operations around Indonesia. On 17 May she was attacked by machine-gun fire from an unidentified aircraft. There were no casualties and it was thought the attack was carried out by revolutionaries opposed to Indonesia's Sukarno government. With the exception of AFFRAY, which sank in April 1951, AUROCHS was the only one of her class not to undergo the streamlining modernisation and was decommissioned in 1966. She arrived at Troon for breaking up the following year.

HMS AUROCHS (Image No: BW9962)

An Early Battle class destroyer she was built by Swan Hunter & Wigham Richardson Limited on the Tyne and commissioned on 14 September 1944. She was the only one of her class to see action in WWII having been deployed to join the British Pacific Fleet. In September 1945 she was present in Tokyo Bay when the Japanese signed the official surrender onboard the battleship USS MISSOURI. In the late 1940s BARFLEUR operated in the Far East with the 19th DF and in the 1950s became Captain (D) of the 3rd DF, operating in the Mediterranean. In 1956 she took part in the Suez operations before being placed in reserve in 1958. She was broken up at Dalmuir, on the Clyde, in 1966.

A Weapon class destroyer built by Yarrow at Scotstoun, she was completed in October 1947. Conceived as a smaller counterpart to the Battle class it was planned to build twenty of the ships, but with the end of the war only four were completed. Between 1958-59 she was converted to a Radar Picket. This involved adding a large mainmast amidships for the Type 965 with an AKE-1 "single bedstead" antenna, with the torpedo tubes replaced by radar offices. On completion of the refit she joined the 2nd DS and then, in 1961, the 5th DS. In August 1962 she was involved in a collision with the frigate URSA and was uneconomic to repair. In October 1963 she arrived at Blyth to be broken up.

An Improved Town class cruiser, BELFAST was built by Harland & Wolff, Belfast, and completed on 3 August 1939 just prior to the start of WWII. In November 1939, on departure from Rosyth, she struck a mine which broke her back - she subsequently spent two years under repair. On return to service she operated on the Arctic convoys and was instrumental in the destruction of the SCHARNHORST during the Battle of North Cape in December 1943. Post war she operated off Korea and underwent an extensive modernisation from 1956-59. She was placed in reserve in 1963, and after a long campaign was, in 1971, eventually preserved as a museum ship on the River Thames, where she remains today.

One of two LST(3)s that were completed as LST(Q) Headquarters ships, BEN LOMOND was laid down as LST 3013 in 1944 by Fairfield Shipbuilding & Engineering Co Ltd, Glasgow. She was completed as LST(Q)2 in November 1945. The LST(Q)s had deckhouses located on the upperdeck. Facilities on the main tank deck accommodated an additional 196 men. There was also provision for a bakery and an increase in refrigerated capacity for fresh food. Four extra distilling plants were added, and the ballast tanks were converted for the storage of fresh water. Post-war she operated as headquarters ship for bacteriological defence trials. She was eventually sold in 1960 and scrapped at Grays, Essex.

A Type 12 Rothesay class ASW frigate, she was built by Harland and Wolff, Belfast, being completed in June 1961. She took part in the Beira patrol in 1966 and from 1969-71 was modernised at Chatham with a new flightdeck and hangar and a new gunnery system. In 1972-73 she undertook Cod War patrols off Iceland and during the Falklands War in 1982 was brought forward from the Standby Squadron and deployed to the West Indies. She was paid off in 1985 and finally sunk as a target on 18 August 1986.

HMS BERWICK (Image No: BWP38)

HMS BILDESTON was the first of the numerically large Ton class to complete and entered service with the original short funnel design. She was built by J.S. Doige (Grimsby) Ltd and completed in April 1953. From 1954-57 she was allocated to the 50th MSS at Port Edgar. Following a 30 month conversion to a minehunter she re-entered service in 1968 with the 1st MCMS. She was present at both the 1969 Western Fleet Review at Torbay and the 1977 Silver Jubilee Fleet Review at Spithead. She operated as part of NATOs STANAVFORCHAN from January 1980 to January 1981, finally paying off in 1986. She was broken up in 1988.

HMS BILDESTON (Image No: BW12194)

A Type 12 frigate completed by Harland and Wolff, Belfast, on 12 August 1958. She initially served in the Mediterranean but spent much of her time in the Far East. She was transferred to the Royal New Zealand Navy in June 1966 to replace the cruiser ROYALIST. She was returned to the RN in 1971 and paid off. From 1974 she was used for trials and in 1977 was fitted with a large mast, in place of the 4.5-inch gun, for target trials. In May 1978 she was towed to St David-on-Forth to be broken up by J.A. White.

A cruiser of 9,550 tons she was launched by Fairfield Shipbuilding & Engineering Co., Govan, in December 1945. Construction was consequently halted, with all three ships of the class undergoing an extensive redesign with revised superstructure and an armament comprising two twin 6-inch turrets and two twin 3-inch mountings. She was eventually completed in March 1961. Between 1965-69 she underwent a conversion into a helicopter carrying cruiser, her aft 6-inch and 3-inch mountings being replaced by a large hangar and flight deck that could accommodate four helicopters. She also had new masts, radar and taller funnels. With improved command facilities she was ideal as a task group flagship. She paid off in 1979 and following a refit in 1980 was placed in the Standby Squadron. She arrived at Cairnryan for breaking up in November 1982.

A Rover class small fleet tanker, she was built by Swan Hunter, Hebburn, and entered service in July 1970. Owing to unsatisfactory performance from the original engines, which had been a political decision, the first three ships in the class were re-engined in 1974. Despite this in auspicious start, the Rover class proved to be very versatile ships remaining in service with the RFA through to 2017 when the last of the class, RFA GOLD ROVER, decommissioned. BLUE ROVER was one of two that were sold for further service overseas. She decommissioned in 1993 and was transferred to Portugal where she was renamed NRP BERRIO and remains in service today (2017).

RFA BLUE ROVER (Image No: BW704233)

A Ham class inshore minesweeper built by Ailsa Shipbuilding Co., Troon, and completed on 21 October 1953. The class was designed to operate in the shallow water of rivers and estuaries. BOTTISHAM was placed in Operational Reserve at Hythe from 1954/55 and following a 1956 refit was returned to reserve at Sheerness (until 1957) and thence to Hythe. In January 1966 she was transferred to the RAF and operated as HMFA 5000. She was returned to RN control in 1971 and sold in November 1973 to Gomba Marina Ltd.

HMS BOTTISHAM (Image No: BW12363)

A Type 12 frigate she was built by Yarrow & Co Ltd, Scotstoun, and completed on 28 September 1961. After work-up she joined the 6th FS and in 1963 was re-allocated to the 30th ES, Home Fleet. In January 1968 she was a member of the inaugural NATO Squadron, formed at Portland comprising BRIGHTON, NARVIK (Norway), HOLDER (USA) and HOLLAND (Netherlands) - this squadron was later to become STANAVFORLANT. From 1968-1971 she underwent a modernisation refit at Chatham, during which she was fitted with a flight deck and hangar. In 1974 she evacuated British nationals from Cyprus following the Turkish invasion and the following year undertook Cod War patrols. In 1981 she arrived at Rosyth for refit prior to lay up in the Standby Squadron at Chatham. While awaiting disposal she was cannibalised for spares to keep her sisters running. She arrived on the Medway on 16 September 1985 to be broken up.

A Centaur class light fleet carrier BULWARK was built by Harland & Wolff, Belfast, being laid down on 10 May 1945 and launched on 22 June 1948. However, she was not commissioned until 4 November 1954. In 1956 she was deployed on Operation Musketeer, the Suez crisis, where she launched up to 600 sorties. In 1958 she underwent conversion to a commando carrier and operated east of Suez prior to returning to the UK following the withdrawal from Aden in 1967. Throughout the 1970s, together with her sister ALBION she was the mainstay of the UK amphibious forces, but was eventually withdrawn from service in 1976 and placed in reserve. Due to delays with the Invincible class she was refitted and returned to service in 1979 as an ASW carrier. She decommissioned in 1981 and finally declared for disposal in 1983. She was towed away for breaking up at Cairnryan in April 1984.

A Bustler class ocean going rescue tug she was one of eight built for the Admiralty by Henry Robb of Leith. Completed in 1942, she accompanied convoys along the West Africa coast and across the Atlantic, providing salvage and towing services to many damaged ships. In December 1945 she was used to tow surrendered German U-Boats into the Atlantic for destruction under Operation Deadlight. Of the many towing operations post war, she was involved in the recovery of SAUMAREZ to Gibraltar after the Corfu Incident and, lost the Brazilian battleship SAO PAULO during an Atlantic gale, while towing her to the UK for breaking up. In 1959 she was transferred to the RFA. In 1973 she was sold to Brodospas Ponuzeca za Spasavanje I Teglenje, Brodova and renamed MOCNI. She was broken up in 1989.

HMS BUSTLER (Image No: BW21914)

Another Ton class minesweeper she was built by Montrose Shipyard Ltd. and completed in April 1954. In May 1954 she joined the Vernon Training Squadron based at Portsmouth, where she remained for her operational career, being involved in minesweeping equipment trials, including helicopter minesweeping trials in the Solent in 1959. 119 Ton class were built, many serving with overseas navies, but ultimately, many spent much of their lives laid up in reserve with very little active service. CAUNTON managed 11 years in service before being paid off in May 1965. In April 1970 she was sold to Metal Recoveries (Newhaven) Ltd for breaking up.

HMS CAUNTON (Image No: BWF405)

One of 96 War Emergency Programme destroyers ordered between 1940 and 1942, she was a 'Ca' class destroyer of the 11th Emergency Programme ordered from J.S. White of Cowes. She was completed on 22 November 1944 and commissioned for service with the 6th DF, Home Fleet, and escorted major warships on operations off Norway and on convoy runs to Russia. In August 1945 she left for the Far East, returning to the UK to pay off in 1946. She remained laid up until 1955 and was then modernised by Thornycroft of Southampton and recommissioned for service in the Far East. From 1966-72 she was further modernised, being fitted with Seacat missiles on an enlarged after deckhouse. She paid off in 1972 and after several years as a museum ship in various locations around the UK, she now forms part of the Chatham Historic Dockyard where she remains as an example of the destroyer.

A light fleet carrier built by Harland and Wolff, Belfast, she was laid down in May 1944 and launched in April 1947, however, her completion was delayed until September 1953. She saw service in Home Waters and the Mediterranean prior to a refit at Devonport in which steam catapults were added. In 1961 she took part in the reinforcement of Kuwait and in 1964 carried Royal Marines to Tanganyika. From late 1965 to early 1970 she was used as an accommodation ship at Devonport and Portsmouth. On 4 September 1972 she was towed from Devonport for breaking up at Cairnryan.

HMS CHASER was one of the numerous LST (3) type Landing Ship (Tank) built during the Second World War. She started life as L3029, being built by Alexander Stephen and launched on 12 January 1945. Post war she was one of many that saw further service and was renamed CHASER in 1947. Latterly she was used as a depot ship for inshore and coastal minesweepers and in 1958 became a submarine support ship. She was sold in 1962 and scrapped La Spezia.

HMS CHASER (Image No: BW20912)

A Ton class minesweeper, she was built at Fleetlands, Gosport and completed in July 1958. She was initially attached to the 104th MSS serving at Malta prior to moving to Singapore in 1959. In the 1960s she operated with both the 6th MSS (62-65) and 9th MSS (65-69) prior to returning to Gibraltar where, following a refit in 1969, she was placed in reserve at Coaling Island. She returned to service in 1971, joining the Fishery Protection Squadron as a replacement for the damaged BELTON. In 1975 she paid off for disposal and was broken up by Tees Marine at Middlesborough in 1977.

HMS CHAWTON (Image No: BW720906)

An Algerine class minesweeper she was built by Harland and Wolff, Belfast and completed in October 1944. She joined the 18th MSF for service in Home Waters conducting minesweeping and convoy escort duties in the North Sea. Post war she continued mine clearance operations until placed in reserve at Devonport in 1947. She was refitted at Liverpool in 1950 and returned to service in 1951. She was attached to the 4th MSF in the Channel Command. Reduced to reserve again in 1954, this time at Chatham, she was placed on the disposal list in 1963 and was broken up at Queensborough the same year.

HMS CHEERFUL (Image No: BW10350)

A Ham class inshore minesweeper, she was built by Jones (Buckie) being completed on 15 July 1953, commissioning at HMS DILIGENCE, Hythe. From 1954-56 she operated with the 232nd MS before being placed in reserve at Rosneath, where the ships were lifted out of the water and stored ashore on covered cradles. She underwent a refit at Portsmouth in 1958 before returning to reserve, this time at Hythe. In December 1965 she was transferred to the RAF at Plymouth, becoming HMFA 5001. On return to the RN in 1971 she was laid up until sold to Gomba Marine in November 1973 for breaking up.

HMS CHELSHAM (Image No: BW14626)

The Type 61 Salisbury class aircraft direction frigate was built by Fairfield Shipbuilding and Engineering Co. Ltd at Govan. She was launched in April 1955 and completed in May 1958. She operated as part of the 4th Frigate Squadron between 1958 and 1963 for both Home and Far East deployments. She was in refit at Chatham 1963-64, before further deployments to the Far East, including four years as Hong Kong guardship, for which role her Type 965 radar was removed and she was fitted with two extra 20mm Oerlikons and a single 40mm Bofors. She returned to the UK in 1976 and was placed in reserve in 1976. In March 1981 she arrived at Queensborough to be broken up.

HMS CHICHESTER (Image No: BW692095)

A 'Ch' class destroyer she was built by Scotts Shipbuilding and Engineering Company, Greenock, and completed in March 1946. Completed too late to see service in WWII she was allocated to the 1st DS in the Mediterranean and operated on the Palestine Patrol, intercepting illegal immigrants heading for the Holy Land. In 1954 she underwent an interim modernisation, receiving Squid AS mortars in lieu of the 4.5-inch gun in 'X' position. She was part of operation Musketeer - the Suez crisis of 1956, after which she was decommissioned in 1957 and placed in extended reserve at Chatham. She was placed on the disposal list the following year and in March 1961 was towed to Messrs T. Young Ltd. at Sunderland for breaking up.

HMS CHIEFTAIN (Image No: BW22803)

A Leander class frigate, CLEOPATRA was built by HM Dockyard Devonport and completed in March 1966. She joined the 2nd DS, in the Far East and then participated in the Beira Patrol. In 1973 she deployed to the Cod Wars. One of the first group of Leanders, she was modernised to carry Exocet missiles at Devonport from July 1973 to December 1975, the first Leander to be so fitted. The 4.5-inch turret was replaced by four Exocet missiles and a quadruple Seacat launcher. Two further Seacat launchers were sited on the hangar roof. The Limbo well was plated over and two sets of STWS were fitted. The enlarged flightdeck meant that she could operate the Lynx helicopter. In 1982 she was fitted with a towed array which saw the forward Seacat, the Type 965 aerial and some superstructure removed to reduce topweight. She paid off in January 1992 and was towed to Alang, India, to be broken up, arriving in January 1994.

HMS CLEOPATRA (Image No: BW682977)

A 'Co' class destroyer built by J.S. White of Cowes and completed in November 1945. In 1946 she joined the 8th DF in the Far East before returning to the UK in 1948. In 1949 she was an attendant destroyer to Home Fleet aircraft carriers and from February 1952 served as a target ship for submarines based at Gosport. She was present at the Coronation Fleet Review in 1953 and in 1954 received an interim modernisation and was fitted for minelaying operations. From 1955 she was attached to the 6th DS on Home/Mediterranean service and in 1959 paid off into reserve at Chatham. Following her sale she arrived at Thos. W. Ward, Grays, Essex, on 2 February 1960 for breaking up.

A Ton class minesweeper she was built by John I. Thornycroft, being completed in August 1958. She served intitially with the 108th MSS in 1958, before being re-allocated to the 7th MSS in the Mediterranean in 1963. In January 1968 she sailed for earthquake relief duties at Sicily. The following year she was placed in reserve at Gibraltar, returning to service in May 1969 as the Solent Division RNR tender and being renamed WARSASH. In 1977 she returned to the operational fleet, under her original name, and was escort to the Royal Yacht BRITANNIA during the Silver Jubilee Fleet Review. She was sold for disposal in 1987 and was towed from Rosyth for breaking up at Cairnryan.

A Bustler class ocean going rescue tug she was built by Henry Robb of Leith and launched as HMRT GROWLER, being completed in 1943. Post war she was variously chartered to Moller Towages Ltd., Hong Kong, in 1947 as CAROLINE MOLLER. In 1952 she was re-chartered by Moller to Hong Kong Salvage & Towage Co. Ltd. as CASTLE PEAK. She returned to the Admiralty in 1954 as RFA GROWLER and following another short charter, as WELSHMAN, was returned in 1963 and renamed CYCLONE. She was laid up at Gibraltar in 1977 and sold for further commercial service in 1983. She was broken up at Karachi in 1985.

One of eight Daring class destroyers for the Royal Navy she built by J.S. White at Cowes and launched in August 1950. She was completed in February 1953 and following initial trials and limited service she was paid off into reserve and cocooned in mid-1954. In January 1956 she commissioned for general Home/Mediterranean service followed by a refit at Portsmouth in 1958. In 1959 she joined the 2nd DS before a further period in reserve. She refitted from 1962-64 and recommissioned for the 23rd ES serving in the West Indies, East Indies, Mediterranean, Far East and Home Waters. She paid off for disposal in 1969 and was sold for breaking up in 1970.

HMS DAINTY (Image No: BW682302)

One of 27 Dark class fast patrol boats - they could be configured either as MTBs or MGBs. As torpedo boats they were armed with a single 40mm gun and four 21-inch torpedoes whilst as gun boats they carried a single 4.5-inch gun and one 40mm gun, though she is seen here without armament. Built by Taylor (Chertsey), she was launched on 4 October 1955. She was sold for commercial service in 1967.

HMS DARK FIGHTER (Image No: BWH999)

The Ham class minesweeper was built by Jones (Buckie), and completed in December 1953. She entered operational reserve at Hythe/Gosport between 1954-55. Following a refit at Chatham she operated with the 120th MSS at Hong Kong. She was placed in operational reserve at Singapore from 1963 before being sold in April 1966 to Kiaw Aik & Co, Jurong, for breaking up.

A County class cruiser built by Devonport Dockyard and launched on 22 October 1927. She was completed in March 1929. She served with the 1st CS in the Mediterranean (1929-32), the 5th CS on the China Station (1932-33) before rejoining the 1st CS in the Mediterranean from 1933-39. She took part in the evacuation of Norway and in June 1940 brought the King of Norway to Britain. She took part in the Dakar operation and patrolled the South Atlantic for raiders. In August 1941 she went north to cover Russian convoys before returning to the South Atlantic, where in November 1942 she sank the German raider ATLANTIS. Following service with the Eastern Fleet and a refit in the UK she ended the war as she started by escorting the King of Norway back to Oslo. In 1947 she replaced FROBISHER as the Cadet Training Ship, retaining only 'A' turret of her original four twin 8-inch guns. She decommissioned in 1953 and was sold for breaking up at Newport in 1954.

Another Daring class destroyer, she was built by J. Brown at Clydebank and launched in June 1950. She was completed in February 1952 and joined the Home Fleet. In 1953 her bows were damaged in a collision with the cruiser SWIFTSURE off Iceland. Following a period in the Mediterranean she returned to Chatham in 1955 prior to operations off Suez during Operation Musketeer in 1956. In 1957 she visited the USA then joined the 5th DS in the Mediterranean. Following a refit at Chatham in the mid-1960s she recommissioned for Home/Far East Service with the 23rd ES. Following a period in reserve at Chatham she recommissioned for Home/Far East service in August 1967. She paid off at Portsmouth in 1969 and was used as a harbour training ship attached to HMS SULTAN until being towed away in 1981 to be broken up on the Medway.

HMS DIAMOND (Image No: BW681195)

One of the 26 strong Leander class DIDO was built by Yarrow Shipbuilders at Scotstoun and launched on 22 December 1961. She was commissioned in September 1963 and saw service with the 21st ES Home Fleet before deploying to the Far East for service with the 22nd and 21st ES. In March 1969 she was attached to the Standing Naval Force Atlantic. She is seen here in her original configuration with a twin 4.5-inch turret forward and two 40mm Bofors on the hangar roof rather than the Seacat missile system, as fitted to later ships during build. From 1975-78 she underwent an ASW conversion at Devonport which saw the forward 4.5-inch turret replaced by an Ikara missile launcher and the Bofors on the hangar roof replaced by two quad Seacat launchers. She was sold to the Royal New Zealand Navy in 1983 and renamed SOUTHLAND. There she continued in service until 1995.

HMS DIDO (Image No: BW672125)

Built by J.S. White of Cowes she was completed in July 1954, one of ten inshore minehunters of the Ley class. These ships were of composite (non-magnetic metal and wood) construction and had less powerful engines than their minesweeping counterparts as they were not required to tow sweep gear. Served as a tender for the Home Station Clearance Diving Team until 1960. Was sold to Pounds of Portsmouth in 1968.

HMS DINGLEY (Image No: BWX9053)

HMS DUNDAS was the first of three Type 14s built for the RN by J.S. White of Cowes. She was laid down on 17 October 1952, launched 25 September 1953 and completed on 9 March 1956. She spent much of her life with the 2nd FS at Portland except for refits (60-61; 67-68 at Gibraltar and 72-73). In May 1976 she was attached to the FPS during the Cod Wars with Iceland. In 1978 she was placed in reserve at Chatham and in 1979 moved to Portsmouth as an Accommodation Ship. She was broken up at Troon in 1983.

HMS DUNDAS (Image No: BWX4933)

A Type 12 frigate, EASTBOURNE was launched by Vickers-Armstrong Ltd, Tyne and completed in January 1958 at Barrow. She was the only one of the Whitby class fitted with stabilisers. She undertook fishery protection duties and served in the Far East. In 1964 she joined the Dartmouth Training Squadron, being fitted with extra deckhouses and boats. In the 1972-73 her turret, mortars and gunnery director were removed. In 1976 she took part in the Cod War off Iceland and was holed in a collision with the gunboat BALDUR. In 1979-80 she was fitted with paddle wheels, in lieu of propellors, for alongside training at Rosyth. She finally decommissioned in 1984 and was broken up at Inverkeithing in March 1985.

Ordered as the LST(3) type landing ship LST 3523, she was built by Davie Shipbuilding and Repairing Co. Ltd., Lauzon, Quebec, and completed in 1945. She was renamed HMS TROUNCER in 1947. She was renamed EMPIRE GULL in 1956 and transferred to the Atlantic Steam Navigation Company in that year, who used the ship to transfer vehicles for the Army from Tilbury to Hamburg, and later Antwerp. In 1961 operation was transferred to the British India Steam Navigation Company before transfer to the Royal Fleet Auxiliary in 1970 for service in the Mediterranean. Latterly she operated the Marchwood - Antwerp and Liverpool - Northern Ireland resupply routes. She paid off in 1978 and was broken up by Recuperaciones Submarinas S.A, Santander, Spain, in 1980.

A Bay class anti-aircraft frigate she was initially ordered as a Loch class anti-submarine frigate to have been named LOCH BRACADALE, however as the emphasis shifted from ASW to AA during the later stages of WWII the ship was re-ordered in 1944 and completed as an AA variant. Built by Smiths Dock at Middlesbrough she was completed January 1946 as ENARD BAY. In January 1946 she sailed for the Mediterranean to join the local Escort Flotilla and was first deployed in the eastern Mediterranean on the interception of merchant ships carrying illegal Jewish immigrants to Palestine. She returned to the UK in 1947 and was placed in reserve at Plymouth. From 1952-53 she served as an initial sea training ship for young RN officers. She was placed on the disposal list in 1956 and was broken up at Faslane from November 1957.

HMS ENARD BAY (Image No: BW08441)

Built by Henry Robb Ltd. at Leith and completed in 1967 to provide initial at sea training for helicopter pilots. She was jointly manned by RN and RFA personnel and was able to accommodate 120 personnel, in addition to her crew, for flying training. She deployed to the South Atlantic during the Falklands War to act as a helicopter support and refuelling ship in San Carlos Water. On her return she had her flightdeck extended to allow operations by Sea King helicopters. Recently, government papers reveal that, during the Cold War she was one of several dispersal locations for government members in the event of nuclear war. Under the codename Python, she would embark her group in either Loch Torridon or Oban. Laid up at Plymouth in 1989 she was sold to Greek commercial interests in 1990. After languishing for six years she was broken up at Alang, India in 1996.

RFA ENGADINE (Image No: BW732858)

One of three Echo class inshore survey craft, she was built by Blackmore and Sons Ltd, Bideford and completed in 1959. She was built for coastal and harbour hydrographic survey operations and had two echo sounders and a sonar for wreck location. She also carried modern radar, wire sweep gear and an echo sounding launch. She was sold to the Marine Society in 1986 for use as a spares source for her sister ECHO, which had also been sold and renamed EARL OF ROMNEY.

HMS ENTERPRISE (Image No: BWX7058)

One of seven Tribal class, or Type 81, general purpose frigates ESKIMO was built by J.S. White of Cowes and completed on 21 February 1963. They were the first RN frigate designed from the outset to operate a helicopter and were fitted with a G6 gas turbine to allow the ships to leave harbour rapidly, before getting up steam. Air-conditioned and intended for operations in the Gulf, ESKIMO served alternately on Home and Middle East deployments from 1964-68. In 1976 she was deployed to the West Indies and in 1979 was placed in the Standby Squadron at Chatham. Two years later she was placed on the disposal list and in January 1986 was towed to Milford Haven to become a target vessel, but was not used as such. She was eventually scrapped in Spain in 1992.

HMS ESKIMO (Image No: BWH286)

Built by Scotts and completed in 1964, she deployed to the Far East as leader of the 26 ES. In 1966 she operated with STANAV-FORLANT (SNFL) and by 1968 was once more east of Suez. From 1973-6 she underwent Ikara conversion at Devonport. In 1978 she was part of 2 FS at Portland. In 1981 she deployed to the Persian Gulf during the Iran-Iraq war before a further spell with SNFL in 1984. In 1986 she became leader of 1 FS. She decommissioned in 1989 and was sold, like her sister AJAX, to Devonport Management Ltd. for modernisation and onward sale to an overseas operator, but this plan fell through and she was scrapped at Millom in 1990.

A Type 14 class frigate she was built by J.S. White at Cowes and launched on 16 November 1955. She was completed on 20 December 1957 and initially employed as a submarine target ship. From December 1963 to March 1966 she was attached to the Fishery Protection Squadron after which she underwent a two year long conversion to the RN's first warship powered entirely by gas turbine. The installation comprised a Bristol Siddeley Olympus for high speeds and two Bristol Siddeley Proteus engines for cruising, all geared to a single shaft. Her external profile was changed by the addition of a large funnel and huge intakes - necessary for the gas turbines huge demand for air. She was placed in reserve in 1976 and towed to Swansea for breaking up in February 1979.

One of a pair of Amphibious Assault ships FEARLESS was built by Harland and Wolff at Belfast and launched on 19 December 1963. She was completed on 25 November 1965. In 1968 she was used as a venue for Rhodesian/UK government talks at Gibraltar and from 1980-81 underwent a commercial refit. She played a crucial role in the 1982 Falklands campaign and by 1983 had resumed her role as Dartmouth Training Ship, a task she alternated with her sister INTREPID. She paid off into reserve in 1985 but recommissioned in 1990, now sporting two Vulcan Phalanx CIWS mounts in place of the elderly Seacat missile launchers. She remained in service until 2002, the last steam-powered surface vessel in the RN. On 17 December 2007 she was towed to Ghent, Belgium, to be broken up.

One of eight County class destroyers, she was built by Fairfield at Govan and launched on 9 July 1964. She was completed in June 1966 and was one of four County class to be fitted with the Exocet missile in place of 'B' turret. In 1979 she was awarded the Wilkinson Sword of Peace for her relief work in the Caribbean after Hurricane David and from 1979-80 was the fleet training ship at Portsmouth. From 1980-83 she was undergoing refit and so missed out on the Falklands War. She was fitted with two triple ASW torpedo tubes and a Lynx helicopter. Following a further refit in 1986 she emerged as a cadet training ship, the Seaslug missile launcher being removed and replaced by a deckhouse containing navigation classrooms. She was decommissioned in 1987 and sold to Chile where she was renamed BLANCO ENCALADA. During her initial refit in Chile her flightdeck was extended aft. She was decommissioned in 2003 and scrapped in 2005.

A Battle class destroyer, she was built by Fairfields of Govan on the Clyde. She was launched on 22 June 1944 and commissioned on 11 September 1945. Following service in both Home Waters and the Far East. In 1952 the ship became the Gunnery Training Ship, based at Whale Island, Portsmouth. Following participation in the 1953 Coronation Fleet Review, she was placed in reserve, but was returned to active service in 1959 to replace her sister ship HOGUE which had been extensively damaged following a collision in the Far East. FINISTERRE was sold for scrap in 1965.

A Ton class minesweeper she was built by Whites at Southampton, being completed in January 1955 after which she was placed in operational reserve at Hythe. From 1960-76 she operated as tender to the Sussex division RNR, being renamed CURZON. In January 1976 she was renamed FITTLETON and attached to the 10th MCMS (Channel). Following Exercise Teamwork 1976, she proceeded in company with six minesweepers towards Hamburg for a three-day visit. During the passage she was detailed to undertake a mail transfer with the frigate MERMAID. During the evolution the ships collided and FITTLETON capsized with the loss of 12 crew, the largest peacetime loss in recent RN history. The wreck was lifted and taken to Chatham. In 1977 it was sold and broken up at Sittingbourne.

Built by Swan Hunter, on the Tyne, and completed in 1964 and immediately stationed in the Mediterranean. She underwent an Ikara conversion from 1971-74 at Devonport. She took part in the Third Cod War with Iceland and was rammed by the ICGV BALDUR. In 1980 she deployed to the Far East and the following year entered refit at Gibraltar. This view shows the cramped flight deck with the small Wasp embarked, astern of which is a three-barreled LIMBO ASW mortar and in the stern cut out, the variable depth sonar. She paid off in 1986 and two years later was towed from Portsmouth to be sunk as a target as part of naval exercises in the North Atlantic.

One of a class of twelve fast patrol boats that served from the early 1950s. The class could be fitted as either motor gun boats or motor torpedo boats, depending on the type of armament they carried. GAY CHARGER was built by Morgan Giles of Teignmouth and launched on 12 January 1953. In May 1954 she escorted the Royal Yacht BRITANNIA from the Nore to the Pool of London and placed in reserve the following year. In 1959 she was converted to a high speed target towing vessel based at Devonport. In 1964 she was paid off for disposal.

A Beachy Head class maintenance ship built by Burrard Dry Dock Co., Vancouver, she was launched in March 1945. She paid off in 1946 and from 1947-53 was in Reserve at Rosyth. From 1953 she underwent a 3-year long conversion at Devonport, emerging in July 1956 as a guided weapons trials ship, mounting a triple-launcher forward for the Seaslug missile system. She spent most of 1959-61 in the Mediterranean as part of the missile trials programme. She was paid off into reserve in 1962 and served as base and accommodation ship at Rosyth until 1970. She arrived at Faslane for breaking up in August 1970.

Ordered as the controlled minelayer M2, she was built by Philip & Son at Dartmouth and completed on 19 January 1940. She was renamed MINER II in 1942 and served throughout the war in Home Waters laying mines to protect ports and shipping channels. Renamed GOSSAMER in 1949 she became a mine location vessel attached to HMS OSPREY at Portland. She was sunk as a target May 1970 by the Iranian destroyer ARTEMIZ (ex-HMS SLUYS).

The Rover class small fleet tankers built for the RFA can refuel a ship on either beam or from a hose trailed astern. A flightdeck aft allows for the vertical replenishment of solid stores by helicopter. Built by Swan Hunter on the Tyne GREEN ROVER was completed in August 1969. In September 1969 she towed the disabled RFA APPLELEAF from the North Atlantic to Devonport and in 1972 was used for Harrier deck landing trials. She was decommissioned in 1992 and purchased by Swan Hunter who subsequently sold her to Indonesia where she serves with their navy as KRI ARUN.

Leader of the eight 'U' class war built destroyers GRENVILLE was built by Swan Hunter and Wigham Richardson, Wallsend, and launched on 12 October 1942. She was completed on 27 May 1943 and saw action during the Anzio landings and was also present at Normandy for the D-day landings. She also saw service east of Suez towards the end of hostilities against the Japanese. In 1953 underwent conversion to a Type 15 anti-submarine frigate completing in 1954. She commissioned as leader of the 2nd TS and four years later transfered to the 5th FS. From 1960-64 she was in reserve at Gibraltar. She was towed to Portsmouth where she was converted to undertake trials for the Admiralty Surface Weapons Establishment (ASWE) during which time she was fitted with additional masts, radar and deckhouses as required for trials. She was placed on the sales list in 1974 and in February 1983 was towed to Queensborough for breaking up.

A Type 14 frigate, HARDY was the first of three such vessels built by Yarrows. She was laid down on 4 February 1953, launched on 25 November that year and completed on 15 December 1955. Her first three years were spent with 3 TS at Londonderry before paying-off for a refit. She then remained at Portland through to July 1975 when she paid off into the Standby Squadron at Chatham, returning to service for short periods from November 1976-July 1977 (Portland Squadron) and October 1977-April 1978 (2 FS Portland). In 1979 she moved to Portsmouth as an accommodation ship and in 1983 was towed from Portsmouth to waters off Gibraltar where she was sunk as a target ship having been hit by multiple Exocet, Sea Skua, gunfire and finally torpedo!

A stores carrier built in 1962 by Henry Robb, she was one of a pair of Admiralty designed vessels chartered specifically for sea freighting duties. They initially maintained a UK - Gibraltar - Malta - Aden - Singapore service and following the closure of the Suez Canal in 1967 they went via the Cape of Good Hope. In November 1978 she was severely damaged following an arson attack whilst berthed at Gibraltar. Declared a constructive total loss her charter was terminated and she was returned to her owners. She was purchased by Greek interests and returned to civilian service and, though she was to have a chequered history, she survived until 1987 finally arriving for breaking up at Cyprus in September.

Initially ordered as a Centaur class light fleet carrier, HERMES was laid down at Vickers-Armstrong on 21 June 1944 but, construction was suspended in 1945. The hull was launched in 1953 to clear the slipway and she was eventually completed, to a much modified design, in November 1959. She served as a conventional fixed-wing aircraft carrier until decommissioning in 1970. She returned to service in 1973 following a conversion to a commando carrier, able to operate troop carrying helicopters, transport landing craft in davits and accommodate 800 troops. By 1976 a smaller refit saw her role change to that of an ASW carrier, replacing her troop carrying helicopters with ASW Sea Kings. In 1981 she emerged from another refit with a 12° ski jump fitted over the bow to enable her to operate the Sea Harrier. The following year, the ship deployed as the flagship of the successful operation to retake the Falkland Islands. She decommissioned in 1984 and was transferred to the Indian Navy in 1987 following a refit at Devonport. Renamed VIRAAT she served until 2017 when replaced by VIKRAMADITYA. There are plans to preserve the ship as a museum in India.

A Ton class minesweeper, she was built by J.I. Thornycroft of Southampton, and completed in June 1955. She was the first of the class to be powered by Napier Deltic lightweight diesel machinery as opposed to the Mirrlees diesels of the earlier ships. She was allocated to the 105th MSS at Harwich before entering operational reserve at Chatham in 1957. She returned to service in 1958, initially with the 50th MSS, which became the 3rd MSS, both at Port Edgar. In July 1963 she took part in Operation Cableway, a joint RN/RNR live minesweeping exercise based at Den Helder, Holland. Following a period in reserve at Gibraltar in 1972, she joined the Fishery Protection Squadron, where she remained until 1975. She decommissioned in 1976 and was sold to Tees Marine, Middlesborough, for breaking up in February 1978.

A fleet aircraft carrier, she was built by Fairfields, Govan, and completed on 28 August 1944. She carried out numerous air strikes on targets in Norwegian waters before being transferred to the British Pacific Fleet in time for air strikes against Truk and the Japanese homelands. Post war meant a period in reserve and under refit before serving for a year (1949-50) as Flagship of the C-in-C Home Fleet. From 1951-54 she was allocated to the training Squadron and was present at the Coronation Fleet Review as Flagship of the Flag Officer, Training Squadron. In 1954 she was reduced to reserve and in November 1955 commenced breaking up at Inverkeithing.

Built as the Ley class inshore minehunter CRADLEY, she was completed by Saunders Roe, being completed in May 1955. They differed from the Ham class minesweepers in being of composite construction instead of all wooden. They featured an extended deckhouse and less powerful engines as they were not required to tow a sweep wire. She was maintained in reserve, land cradled at Hythe, until 1963 when she was allocated to the London division RNR and renamed ISIS. From 1974 to 1981 she was attached to Southampton University RN Unit. She was sold in 1982 to Pounds of Portsmouth.

An Algerine class minesweeper, she was built by Harland and Wolff, Belfast and completed in December 1944. From 1945-46 she served in the Far East before returning to the UK to be placed in reserve at Portsmouth. In 1948 she was attached to Tay division RNVR. The ship was brought forward from reserve in 1955 and refitted at Devonport to recommission for service in the Dartmouth Training Squadron. She was deployed for training of cadets from the Royal Naval College at Dartmouth until 1961 when she was placed in reserve. Placed on the Disposal List in 1966 she was sold to BISCO and towed to Inverkeithing for demolition where she arrived in April 1967.

A 1943 or Later Battle-class fleet destroyer, she was built by Alex Stephen and Sons Ltd. at Govan and completed in July 1947. Originally named MALPLAQUET she was renamed before launch. In 1947 she was attached to the 4th DF Home Fleet and was placed in reserve in 1953. She recommissioned in May 1958 and was allocated to the 7th DS. She paid off in 1962 for disposal, arriving at Blyth to be broken up in May 1965.

A Type 14 frigate KEPPEL was built by Yarrows, Scotstoun and completed on 6 July 1956. Until 1958 she served with the Londonderry Squadron after which she paid off into refit. In September 1960 she was attached to the Portland Squadron and from June 1963 - April 1964 operated with the FPS. From May 1967 she was once again at Londonderry prior to moving to Rosyth from where she operated November 1969 - October 1972. In 1973 she was placed in the Standby Squadron at Chatham. In July 1975 she joined 2 FS at Portland until November 1976. She was placed on the Disposal List in 1977 and on 18 April 1979 was towed from Portsmouth to be broken up by Liguria Marine Ltd. at Sittingbourne, Kent.

A Castle class corvette, these ships were built to a prefabricated design, allowing parts to be built around the country and construction to be undertaken by smaller shipbuilders, thereby allowing the larger yards to concentrate on the larger ships and, in this way, keeping the national shipbuilding capacity fully extended. KNARESBOROUGH CASTLE was built by Blyth Shipbuilding and Dry Dock Company Ltd., being launched in September 1943 and completed in April 1944. She was allocated to the B3 EG and in 1944 became senior officer of the B23 EG engaged on the UK-Gibraltar run. By the end of the war she was operating with the Liverpool Escort Pool. Post war she was allocated to Air Sea Rescue duties based initially at Gibraltar and then Freetown before returning to the UK and reducing to reserve at Harwich. In 1952 she was recommissioned for service with the 2nd TS at Portland and was present at the Coronation Fleet Review at Spithead in 1953. In reserve in 1955 she was sold in 1956 and arrived at Port Glasgow March 1956 to be broken up by Smith and Houston Ltd.

A Bay class frigate, she was built by Pickersgill, Sunderland, and completed in January 1946. The ship was originally ordered on 25 January 1943 as the Loch class frigate LOCH FOIN, and laid down on 8 February 1944. However, the contract was subsequently changed, and the ship was completed to a revised design as a Bay class anti-aircraft frigate. After sea trials she sailed for the Mediterranean, joining the Escort Flotilla at Malta in 1946, operating in the eastern Mediterranean intercepting merchant ships bound for Palestine. She returned to the UK to decommission in August 1946 and was placed in reserve. In 1952 she was allocated to the 4th TS based at Rosyth and attended the 1953 Coronation Fleet Review before, once more, entering reserve in 1954. She was placed on the Disposal List in 1958, and arrived at Inverkeithing in July 1959 for demolition by Thos. W. Ward.

The nameship of her class, she was originally laid down, by Harland and Wolff, as the Type 12 frigate WEYMOUTH. She was launched on 28 June 1961 and completed as LEANDER in March 1963. From 1964-67 she deployed to the West Indies and the Far East. From 1970-72 she was converted, at Devonport, to carry the Ikara missile system. On returning to the fleet she was allocated to the 3rd FS and operated in the Indian Ocean, Far East and South America. From December 1975 she deployed to waters off Iceland during the Third Cod War. She was rammed by ICGV THOR in January 1976, causing such serious damage, that she had to return to the UK for repairs. During the transit she broke down in severe gales and was escorted back by BACCHANTE. A further refit at Devonport, from 1976-77 was followed by service in the Mediterranean and Baltic. She paid off into reserve in July 1986 and was sunk as a target in 1989.

A Castle class corvette, she was built by William Pickersgill, Sunderland, and completed in February 1944. She served with the B3 Escort Group and was employed on escort duties and patrol work protecting Atlantic convoys until the end of WWII. Post-war she was attached to the 2nd TS at the Portland until paid off at Chatham in November 1956. She was broken up at Grays, Essex, in 1958.

A Ton class minesweeper, she was built by Harland and Wolff, Belfast, and completed on 29 June 1955. She was allocated to the 104th MSS based at Harwich. Following exercises and port visits in Home and Northern European waters, in 1956 she was deployed to the Mediterranean and took part in Operation Musketeer during the Suez crisis. From 1957-64 she was in reserve at Hythe before returning to service in 1964. In January 1965 she joined the Fishery Protection Squadron to replace WATCHFUL (ex-BROOMLEY), but retained her own name. She remained with the FPS until she paid off in August 1969. In June 1971 she was sold to C. H. Rugg, Belgium for breaking up.

Ordered in 1942 as the Minotaur class cruiser DEFENCE she was built by Scotts Shipbuilding and Engineering Company, Greenock, and launched on 2 September 1944. With the end of the war, construction halted. She was completed by Swan Hunter and Wigham Richardson, to a revised design, on 20 July 1960 and renamed LION. The modified design saw the original armament replaced by rapid fire automatic 3-inch and twin 6-inch gun turrets. From 1963-64 she was Flagship of Flag Officer Flotillas Home Fleet. In September 1964 she was present at the Maltese Independence celebrations after which she was placed in reserve at Devonport from 1964 until 1972. A planned conversion to a helicopter cruiser, as her sisters, TIGER and BLAKE was cancelled and she instead became a source of spares for the remaining pair. She was laid up at Rosyth in 1973 and in February 1975 was towed to Inverkeithing for breaking up.

A Loch class anti-submarine frigate she was built by Harland and Wolff, Belfast, and completed in July 1945. On completion of work up she sailed for the East Indies, returning to the UK to enter reserve in November 1947. Following a refit at Sheerness she recommissioned into the 6th Frigate Flotilla in 1950 serving in Home Waters. In 1955 she commissioned once again for the East Indies station remaining there until paying off for refit at Portsmouth in 1960. A further four years in the East Indies followed before paying off for disposal at Portsmouth in August 1965. She arrived at Blyth to be broken up in March 1970.

A Type 12, or Rothesay class frigate, she was built by J.S. White of Cowes and launched on 20 May 1958. She was completed in July 1960. From 1960-67 she served in Home, West Indies and Far East. She underwent a modernisation refit at Portsmouth from 1967-69, emerging with a flightdeck and hangar which enabled her to operate a Wasp helicopter. Between 1975 and 1979 she was refitted at Rosyth for service as a trials ship for ASWE. She had her armament removed and additional masts and deckhouses fitted for trialling various radars. In early 1982 she accompanied FEARLESS on a training cruise to the West Indies and America after which she paid off into reserve. With the advent of the Falklands War, she was returned to service as part of the Dartmouth Training Squadron before paying off in 1984 to become harbour training ship for HMS SULTAN at Gosport. She remained in this role until 1988. On 25 June 1989 she was sunk as a target off Scotland.

HMS LONDONDERRY (Image No: BWH296)

A Ness class stores support ship, she was built by Swan Hunter and Wigham Richardson and launched on 7 April 1966. Completed in December the same year, she was one of three ships designed as floating supermarkets. Carrying everything from general naval stores including stocks of clothing, mess gear and medical supplies, together with dry and refrigerated food they enabled the fleet to remain at sea for considerable periods. One of the ships, STROMNESS was stored as an air stores support ship carrying over 80,000 items of aircraft stores to meet the needs of the carriers. With the demise of the carriers LYNESS found herself without a role and was chartered to the US Military Sealift Command in 1981 and renamed USNS SIRIUS. She was purchased outright in 1982 and was fitted with a hangar complex to allow her to accommodate two helicopters. She paid off into reserve in 2005. She was intended to be converted to a training ship but these plans fell through and she arrived at Esco Marine Inc, Texas, in May 2014 to be broken up.

RFA LYNESS (Image No: BW670920)

A Type 41, or Leopard class, anti-aircraft frigate, she was built by John Brown at Clydebank, being launched on 12 January 1955. She was completed in March 1957 and up to 1962 operated with the 7th FS at Home and in the South Atlantic. She underwent a refit at Portsmouth from 1962-63 receiving new radar and plated in masts to support the new weight. This was followed by more deployments to the South Atlantic (1963) and Far East (1967). She paid off into the Standby Squadron at Chatham in 1974. The Type 41s were powered by diesel rather than steam and as such had a rather extended range of operations, which suited their role of AA defence for convoys. However, their low speed prevented them from operating with the fleet. She was sold to Bangladesh in 1982 and renamed ABU BAKR. She was decommissioned in January 2014 and had been scrapped by 2017.

An Algerine class minesweeper she was built by Port Aurthur Shipyards, Canada and completed on 21 November 1944. She was attached to the 11th MSF until January 1947 when she paid off into reserve at Singapore. She recommissioned in March 1950 and was allocated as RNVR ship at Hong Kong and renamed CORNFLOWER. She served with the 6th MSEF at Singapore prior to arriving at Sheerness for a refit in 1954. The following year she became a training ship with the VERNON squadron prior to being placed in reserve in 1956 at Chatham. She arrived at Blyth to be broken up in November 1957.

A River class frigate, she was built by Inglis at Glasgow, being completed in December 1943. In April the following year she was loaned to the Royal Canadian Navy and served in the 9th Support and Escort Group. Between April and December 1945 she was converted to a Landing Ship Headquarters (Small) at Southampton. She was commissioned as HQ ship for the Amphibious Warfare Squadron in the Persian Gulf and remained there until 1965 when she returned to Portsmouth to pay off. In May 1966 she left Portsmouth under tow to be broken up at Blyth.

HMS MEON (Image No: BWX3070)

HMS MERMAID was laid down by Denny in September 1942, launched in November the following year and completed in March 1944. Following work-up she sailed with her first Arctic convoy (JW59) in August 1944, during which she sank U-354. On the return trip a further U-boat, U-394, was sunk. There followed operations around the Clyde and Scapa Flow bases and, after a refit at Leith which lasted until March 1945, she joined the 12th EG based at Liverpool. On completion of the war she saw extended service with the Mediterranean Fleet not returning to Portsmouth until 1954, whereupon, she reduced to reserve. She was sold in 1957 to the Bundesmarine recommissioning two years later as FGS SCHARNHORST. She survived until 1990 as a static Damage Control Hulk, before being towed away for breaking up at Bruges.

HMS MERMAID (Image No: BW10396)

An Admiralty type 126ft wooden motor minesweeper, MMS1044 was built at Wivenhoe Shipyard, Essex, and completed on 2 August 1944. She was one of 96 such vessels built in Britain between 1943-45. Standard armament comprised two single 20mm Oerlikons. They were fitted with a variety of Oropesa, magnetic and acoustic sweeps. After sweeping duties in Europe MMS 1044 was transferred, on loan, to the Danish Navy from June 1945 to November 1950. She was returned to the RN and placed in reserve at Chatham and remained there until 1952 when she moved to Portsmouth. She was re-allocated to Chatham in 1953 until sold out of service in November 1954.

A Fairmile B Motor Launch she was ordered in August 1940 as ML342 from Johnson and Jago, Leigh-on-Sea and commissioned on 10 October 1941. Designed for coastal operations around 650 Fairmile 'B' MLs were built and operated by Commonwealth and Allied navies. Of wooden construction they were originally intended for AS operations and equipped with ASDIC and armed with depth charges and a single 3-pdr gun. As the war progressed some were fitted with torpedo tubes and gun armament was increased as new roles were found. Post-war she was renamed ML 2342 and converted to operate in the minesweeping role, being fitted with davits and minesweeping gear as seen here. Though many vessels found further use in the private sector, particularly as pleasure boats, ML2342 was sold on 26 November 1962 for breaking up.

A Moor class mooring vessel she was built by Goole Shipbuilding & Repairing Co. Ltd., being launched on 16 September 1943. The ship was fitted with salvage pumps, air compressors and diving equipment for use as a salvage vessel. She was sold in September 1962 to Davies and Newman for breaking up.

HMS MURRAY was a Type 14 frigate built by Alex Stephen & Sons, Govan. She was laid down on 30 November 1953, launched on 25 February 1955 and completed on 5 June 1956. Except for a modernisation refit at Rosyth from 1962-63, she operated with 2 FS at Portland through to July 1969. In 1960 she was attached to the FPS for operations off Iceland during the Cod War and the Christchurch Times of 13 May 1960 records that, on her return from Iceland, via a visit to Norway, she was the first warship to visit the south coast town since shortly after the Second World War. She was the first post-war frigate to go to the breakers, arriving at Dalmuir in September 1970.

An Algerine class minesweeper she was built by Harland and Wolff, Belfast, and launched in October 1942. Completed on 26 February 1943 she was assigned to the 12th MSF and was initially deployed to Home waters prior to transferring to the Mediterranean in May the same year. She supported the Allied landings at Salerno. Further sweeping operations in the Adriatic and Aegean followed. In December 1944, together with sisters FLY and ALBACORE, she swept a passage through the Dardenelles to ensure a safe passage for the warships taking Churchill and Roosevelt to the Yalta Conference. MUTINE remained in the Mediterranean until returning to the UK in 1946. She was paid off at Sheerness and placed in reserve at Harwich.She recommissioned in April 1956 as a minesweeper training vessel at Portsmouth. Following a further period in reserve at Chatham she was refitted for use as an ASW escort but never served as such being put up for disposal in 1966. She was broken up at Barrow-in-Furness, arriving on 7 April 1967.

An 'O' class destroyer, she was built by Denny at Dumbarton and completed in September 1942. She operated with the Home Fleet escorting convoys to Russia and in December was damaged by the German heavy cruiser LÜTZOW. In January 1944 she was further damaged, south of Bear Island, by a Gnat torpedo fired from U-360. Post war the ship was used for training before being placed in reserve at Portsmouth in 1948. Following a refit on the Tyne she returned to reserve at Chatham from 1950-52. She recommissioned in 1952 and was allocated to the Nore local squadron. Following a further period in reserve (1957-59) she was allocated to the Naval Construction Research Establishment at Rosyth for destructive tests. She was sold for scrap in 1964, arriving at Inverkeithing in November 1964.

An Oberon class submarine, she was built by Cammell Laird and completed in February 1963. Although similar in outward appearance to the earlier Porpoise class, the Oberons had many improvements including a glass fibre conning tower, higher grade steel in hull construction (QT28 vice UXW steel) and an improved equipment fit. Decommissioned in 1993, ORACLE arrived at Pounds Yard, Portsmouth for breaking up in 1993.

HMS ORACLE (Image No: BWN456)

A 73ft Type II Motor Torpedo Boat she was built by Vosper at Portchester. Ordered in December 1943, she was commissioned in July 1945. Based upon the hull of the previous group this vessel had an improved armament - the original twin 20mm Oerlikon was resited aft while a potent 6-pdr 7cwt MkIIA gun, on a power operated mounting, was sited forward of the bridge. The torpedo tube armament was reduced to the after pair. Post war the forward mounting was removed and she was renumbered P1023. On 18 May 1953, while moored alongside GAY ARCHER and two other coastal craft at Aarhus, Denmark, the vessel suffered an explosion and subsequent fire while refuelling with volatile 100-octane aviation spirit. She burned ferociously and subsequently sank in the harbour - GAY ARCHER also suffered significant fire damage before managing to extract herself from P1023.

HMS P1023 (Image No: BW9911)

An Improved Fairmile D type Motor Torpedo Boat she was originally built by A.M. Dickie and Sons, Bangor, North Wales, as MTB 5010 and completed in January 1945. Nicknamed "Dog Boats", they were designed to combat the known advantages of the German E-boats over previous British coastal craft designs. At 115ft in length, they were bigger than earlier MTB or Motor Gun Boat (MGB) designs (which were typically around 70 feet) but slower, at 30 knots compared to 40 knots. A total of 209 were built during the war and they proved to be the most heavily armed units for their size. The early boats mounted four 18-inch torpedo tubes, whereas the later units, such as 5010 carried a pair of heavier 21-inch. Gun armament comprised a 6-pdr and 20mm guns together with depth charges. Post war she was renumbered P3050 and in 1953 was converted to a Motor Anti-Submarine Boat (MASB). She was sold in July 1955.

An earlier Fairmile D she was classed as a combined MGB/MTB and ordered as MTB 779 from Woodnutt & Co Ltd, St Helens, Isle of Wight, and completed in October 1944. By late 1946 only about two dozen Dog boats survived in service - many had been sold out of service as houseboats for around £500 after being stripped of armament and engines, whilst others were loaned to Sea Cadet Units. MTB 779 was renumbered P5032 in 1949 and sold in 1955.

Ordered as CT101 she was one of four Control Target Boats built by J.S. White & Co., Cowes. She was completed on 11 November 1947. These craft were designed to tow targets at speed and also to control remotely operated target boats (Radio Control Boats - RCBs). The majority of such vessels were conversions of surplus MTB/MGBs, but these were new build and designed for the purpose.

Ordered as MTB 521 she was built by British Power Boat (Hythe) and completed in November 1946. She could be armed with torpedo tubes for the MTB role or fitted as a Motor Gun Boat as required. She survived the war and served in the post-war RN as a Radio Control Target Boat (RCB 3). They were crewed during transit between operating bases and target areas, but operated unmanned and controlled by a Control Target Boat once in exercise areas. She ended her service as P8203 (ex CT8203) and was sold in 1958.

A 'P' class destroyer she was built at Chatham Dockyard and completed in December 1941. She took part in Operation Ironclad, the capture of Diego Saurez in May 1942, the Vigorous and Harpoon convoys to Malta and in actions against enemy surface units in the Mediterranean. She helped sink U-205 off Libya in 1943 and the Japanese submarine I-27 in the Indian Ocean in 1944. She left the East Indies Station in October, arriving in Portsmouth in November 1945 and was placed in reserve at Harwich in 1947. From 1952-54 she was converted to a Type 16 A/S frigate at Rosyth. After trials she was once more placed in reserve until 1958 when she recommissioned for service, based at Chatham. She was placed on the Disposal List in June 1961 and the following year sold to Clayton & Davie for breaking up, where she arrived on 25 October 1962.

A Modified Black Swan class sloop, she was built by Thornycroft, Woolston, and completed in May 1944. She joined the 22nd EG and assisted in the sinking of three U-Boats; U-354 (24.8.44), U-394 (2.9.44) and U-482 (16.1.45). In 1945 she joined the 2nd FF in the Mediterranean, returning to Portsmouth in August 1954 to pay off into reserve. She was placed on the disposal list in 1958 and in May that year arrived at Rosyth to be broken up.

HMS PELLEW was the first of a pair of Type 14 frigates built by Swan Hunter on the Tyne. She was laid down on 5 November 1953, launched on 29 September 1954 and completed on 7 February 1957. Her short career was spent with 2 TS and 2 FS at Portland except for a refit from 1961-62 at Rosyth. She was paid off at Portsmouth in April 1969 and on 17 May 1971 arrived at Fleetwood to be broken up.

A Colossus class light fleet aircraft carrier, the ship was initially named EDGAR, but was renamed in 1944 when the Admiralty decided to convert her to an aircraft maintenance carrier. She was built by Vickers-Armstrongs, Newcastle-upon-Tyne, and completed in August 1945. After a spell of duty with the British Pacific Fleet she paid off into reserve at Portsmouth in 1946. From 1949-51 she was refitted and equipped with a steam catapult for trials and development. Following these trials, she was, in 1953, redesignated a ferry carrier. She was further refitted in 1955 but then reduced to reserve. In May 1958 she was sold to Smith & Houston to be broken up at Port Glasgow.

An Algerine class minesweeper, she was built by Harland and Wolff, Belfast, and completed in October 1943. On completion she was based at Tobermory and in 1944 joined the 7th MSF. She operated in European waters until March 1945 and was present at the D-Day landings. In 1945 she deployed to the Far East, returning to the UK in 1946 and being placed in reserve at Plymouth. In 1951 she was moved to Harwich and after a brief spell in commission in 1953-54 returned to reserve at Portsmouth. In 1958 she was towed from Portsmouth to Devonport and sold to Ceylon, being handed over on 6 April 1959 and being renamed PARAKRAMA. She was broken up in 1964.

A coastal minelayer she was built by William Denny and Bros, Dumbarton and commissioned in September 1937. Designed to carry 100 mines, at the outbreak of WWII she started to lay mines in the Straits of Dover, eventually laying over 15,000 mines throughout the war, which she ended in the Far East as part of the British Pacific Fleet. Returning to the UK in 1946 she was assigned as tender to HMS VERNON for duty as a minelaying trials tender until placed on the Disposal List in 1967. She was sold to Thos. W. Ward in 1969 and scrapped at Inverkeithing.

A Modified Black Swan class sloop, she was built by Yarrows, Scotstoun, and completed in June 1943. From 1943-44 she operated in the Atlantic as a convoy escort and in June 1944 covered movements of assault convoys during Operation Neptune. In September 1944 she was headed for operations with the Eastern Fleet and assisted in the assault on Ramree Island, Burma. After service with the British Pacific Fleet the ship returned to the UK in 1946 and was placed in reserve at Harwich. In 1949 the ship was refitted for duty as Navigation Training Ship attached to HMS DRYAD at Portsmouth. In 1958 the ship was placed in reserve, where she remained until 1960. She was sold for demolition by J.A. White, St Davids, arriving under tow on 20 November that year.

Another Harland and Wolff built Algerine, she was completed in June 1943 and commissioned for service with the 19th MSF based at Port Edgar on the Firth of Forth. From 1944 she was operating in the Mediterranean and Adriatic and participated in the Anzio landings. From 1945 she was based at Taranto for mine clearance operations to provide clear passage to Trieste and Genoa. She returned to the UK in 1946 and was placed in reserve at Portsmouth. In May 1951 she joined the 4th MSS at Harwich for minesweeping training and Home Fleet duties. She remained in service until 1955 when she was reduced to Reserve at Portsmouth where she remained until placed on the Disposal List in 1961. The ship arrived at C.W. Dorkin, Sunderland, to begin breaking up on 12 August 1961.

A coastal stores carrier, she was built by Grangemouth Dockyard and completed in 1938. She had a large No2 hold which could accommodate anything used in the Services, including landing craft. She entered RFA service in 1940 and served in the Mediterranean and at the Normandy landings. Post war she operated, in the main, around the UK coast but occasionally ventured as far afield as Malta. She was laid up at Chatham in 1971 and offered for sale in March 1972. She arrived at Grays, Essex, in June 1972 for demolition by T.W. Ward Ltd.

A Type 61 or Cathedral class aircraft direction frigate she was built by HM Dockyard Devonport and launched on 25 June 1953. She was completed on 27 February 1957 and between 1957 and 1967 served in Home, Mediterranean and Far East theatres. In June 1964 she was involved in a collision with the destroyer DIAMOND. From 1967-70 she underwent a modernisation refit receiving plated-in masts to support more powerful radar aerials. A Seacat missile launcher replaced the twin 40mm gun mount aft. In 1976 she was damaged during the Cod War following a collision with TYR and a further two with AEGIR. She was laid up at Chatham in 1978 before being moved to Devonport in 1980 where she served as a Harbour Training Ship. On 30 September 1985 she was sunk west of Ireland as a target.

A Bustler class fleet tug, she was built by Henry Robb at Leith and completed in September 1942. These were the first fleet tugs to be powered by diesel, giving them a speed of 16 knots. Designed for sea towing, salvage and rescue, they were not suitable for harbour work. From 1947-52 she was on charter and named FOUNDATION JOSEPHINE. In 1958 she was Portsmouth manned and in March that year towed HMS/M TURPIN with engine defects from Kingston, Jamaica to Devonport - the tow, 5,200 miles, took 29.5 days which became the longest tow in submarine history, and they arrived on 8 April 1958. The ship was transferred to the RFA in May 1960. In 1973 she was offered for sale and was eventually sold in 1974 to a company in Split and renamed JAKI. She was removed from the register in 1979 and broken up at Split in 1987.

An 'S' class destroyer she was built by Hawthorn Leslie, Hebburn, and completed on June 1943. Unlike her sisters, she was completed with 4.5-inch guns rather than 4.7-inch. The forward mounting was a twin, the prototype for the Battle class. During WWII she operated in the Mediterranean and Arctic, participating in the Battle of North Cape in December 1943. Post war she was deployed as a Gunnery Firing Ship at Portsmouth before being reduced to reserve at Chatham in 1948. She was recommissioned in 1950 for trials of new shaft and propeller designs. She was placed on the disposal list in 1960 and arrived at Newport to be broken up on 11 April that year.

A Type 12, or Whitby, class frigate she was built by Vickers Armstrong on the Tyne and launched in April 1955. She was completed in May 1957 and was the first to be fitted with AS torpedo tubes (four on each side and two swivel mountings). They proved unsuccessful in service and future ships were not fitted and earlier ships had them removed. SCARBOROUGH was unique in that she retained the original small upright funnel throughout her service. Until 1962 she was deployed on Home, Mediterranean and Far East service. She underwent a refit from 1962-64 at Portsmouth before returning to service as a member of the Dartmouth Training Squadron. She paid off in 1972 and was laid up at Devonport. She was towed to the Tyne in March 1973 for a survey by Swan Hunter Shipbuilders and returned the same month. In 1974 a proposed sale to Pakistan was cancelled and in 1977 the ship left the Tyne, where she had been laid up for several months, and was towed to Blyth Shipbreaking & Repairers for breaking up.

A Group III 'S' class submarine she was built by Cammell Laird and completed on 16 March 1945. She had six torpedo tubes and a 4-inch gun, earlier units had an extra torpedo tube aft and a smaller gun. Post war she was attached to the 2nd Submarine Flotilla based on MAIDSTONE. She took part in the search for the missing submarine AFFRAY in 1951 and attended the Fleet Review in 1953. Her gun was removed and she was fitted with a snort mast. Her hull was used for experiments in 1961 and she was broken up at Charlestown in 1962.

A Halcyon class sloop, she was built by Caledon Shipbuilding Co., Dundee and completed in February 1939 as a survey vessel, though converted to a minesweeper in late 1939. By May 1940 she was converted back to a survey vessel and spent much of the next two years employed on mining, providing precise positioning for the minelayers as well as surveying intended minefield sites. She also provided survey and positioning information for the Mulberry Piers during the Normandy landings and subsequently conducted surveys of liberated ports and their approaches. Post-war she was employed on general hydrographic duties in Home Waters, locating and sweeping many of the war-time wrecks and re-surveying large areas off the coast of Great Britain. She arrived at Portsmouth to pay off in November 1964. In June 1965 she was sold to West of Scotland Shipbreaking for breaking up at Troon where she arrived on 3rd July 1965.

HMS SCOTT (Image No: BWX4116)

An 'S' class submarine, she was built by Vickers Armstrong, Barrow, and completed in June 1942 as P219. She was one of the 50 strong Third Group of 'S' class submarines, being larger and more heavily armed than their predecessors. She was assigned to the 8th Flotilla in the Mediterranean. SERAPH was selected to conduct several special operations including landing key officers on the North African coast prior to the Torch landings and picking up General Henri Giraud and entourage from Toulon for talks to enlist the support of pro-Vichy forces at Oran and Casablanca. In 1943 she landed "Major Martin" on the Spanish coast - The Man Who Never Was. Later that year she was a beacon vessel during the Husky landings. She was involved in early streamlining experiments to improve underwater speed and in 1947 she was refitted for use as a submarine target vessel. She paid off in 1963 and arrived at Briton Ferry in December 1965 to be broken up.

HMS SERAPH (Image No: BWX507)

HMS SHACKLETON started her career as the Halcyon class minesweeper SHARPSHOOTER, being built at Devonport and completed in December 1937. Post war she was one of two surplus Halcyon class converted to surveying duties, being shorn of all armament in the process. She served in the Singapore area from 1946-47 before returning to the UK. On 1 July 1953, she was renamed SHACKLETON - a more appropriate name for a survey ship. She paid off at Devonport in November 1962 and languished in reserve until November 1965 when she was sold to the West of Scotland Ship Breaking Company and broken up at Troon.

A Town class cruiser she was built by Vickers Armstrong, completing in August 1937. She served in the Home and Mediterranean Fleets throughout the war, taking part in actions which resulted in the sinking of the German warships BISMARCK, FRIEDRICH ECKHOLDT and SCHARNHORST. She also covered convoys to Malta and Russia. Post-war she served three commissions as Flagship of the C-in-C America and West Indies Station and one commission as Flagship of the Flag Officer, Heavy Squadron, Home Fleet. In 1956-57 she was refitted with an enclosed bridge, lattice foremast and improved AA fire-control. She was in reserve at Portsmouth from 1960. She was broken up at Faslane in 1967

One of six Round Table class logistic landing ships SIR GERAINT was built by Alexander Stephen and Sons Ltd of Linthouse, being launched in January 1967. Completed in July 1967, she was placed under the management of the British India Steam Navigation Company in their corporate livery of white hull with a blue band and buff funnel (as seen here). It was not until March 1970 that they were transferred to the Royal Fleet Auxiliary and adopted the more familiar all-over grey appearance. She was equipped with bow and stern loading facilities for tanks and military vehicles, ramp loading hatches, cargo handling cranes and provision for carrying and launching pontoons. Helicopters could be operated from flight decks aft or over the tank deck. RFA SIR GERAINT operated out of Marchwood Military Port in Southampton. On 28 March 1970 she sailed with RFA EMPIRE GULL from Tobruk for the final withdrawal of British Forces from Libya. She saw service in the South Atlantic during the Falklands War, in 1982, and was decommissioned in 2003. She was broken up in 2005 at Gadani Beach, Pakistan.

A Ton class minesweeper she was ordered as BRERETON from Richards of Lowestoft and completed in July 1954. She was re-named ST DAVID in 1954 when she became a tender to the South Wales unit of the Royal Naval Reserve. She served as such until November 1961 when she reverted to her original name. She replaced SQUIRREL in the Fishery Protection Squadron in 1965 prior to entering refit at Portsmouth in 1967 to undergo conversion to a minehunter. She operated with both the FPS and 10th MCMS squadron prior to decommissioning. She was broken up at Bruges in 1992.

An Early Battle class destroyer, she was built by Swan Hunter, Wallsend, and completed on 21 January 1946. She joined the 5th DF of the Home Fleet and 1948 deployed to the Arctic to conduct cold weather experiments in the region. In 1954 she was allocated to the 3rd DF and in 1956 took part in operations off Suez. She was decommissioned in 1957 and was sold to T. Young, arriving at Sunderland for breaking up on 14 February 1962.

An Isles class minesweeping trawler she was built by J. Lewis and Sons Ltd. of Aberdeen, and launched on 15 July 1943. One of a class of 197 such vessels built for the Royal Navy, Royal Canadian Navy and Royal New Zealand Navy between 1939-45, they were generally similar to the Dance, Tree and Shakespearian classes. STEEPHOLM was commissioned on 1 December 1943 and survived the war. Post war she was one of seventeen of the class to be disarmed and converted to Wreck Disposal Vessels, operated around the coastline to clear coastal waters and port approaches of the wreckage left from WWII. She was scrapped 18 June 1960.

A 'T' class destroyer she was built by Cammell Laird and Co. Ltd., Birkenhead, and completed in September 1943. She joined the 24th DF in the Mediterranean and took part in the landings in South France in August 1944. In 1945 she transferred to the Pacific Fleet, returning to the UK in 1946 when she was placed in reserve at Plymouth. From 1953-54 she was converted to a Type 16 AS frigate at Cardiff and in 1958 recommissioned for service with the 2nd TS. She was placed in reserve in 1961 and de-equipped at Chatham. She arrived at Dalmuir to be broken up in August 1965.

HMS TEAZER (Image No: BW22718)

A Whitby-class or Type 12 anti-submarine frigate, TENBY was built by Cammell Laird and Co. Ltd., Birkenhead, and completed in December 1957. She was allocated to the 5th FS Home and Mediterranean and following a refit period (1958-59) served both at Home and in the Far East. From 1962-72 she was an integral part of the Dartmouth Training Squadron before entering reserve at Devonport. A proposed sale to Pakistan was cancelled and in 1977 she was sold and towed to Briton Ferry for breaking up.

HMS TENBY (Image No: BW702818)

A Colossus class aircraft carrier, she was built by Fairfields, Govan, and completed in January 1946. In 1947 she was Flagship of Flag Officer (Air) in the Far East followed by duty as Flagship of the 3rd Aircraft Carrier Squadron. She was engaged in operations against Chinese forces in the Korean War until 1952 when she became Flagship of the Flag Officer, heavy Squadron and Flag Officer Commanding 2nd Aircraft Carrier Squadron Home Fleet. In 1954 she joined the Training Squadron and was placed in reserve in 1958. She was de-equipped at Chatham and broken up at Inverkeithing in 1962.

Built by Hawthorn Leslie and Co. Ltd., Newcastle she was completed in 1963, one of a pair of Improved Tide class tankers. These ships incorporated a flightdeck and hangar to operate ASW helicopters. During the 1970s the ship took part in both the Cod Wars and the Beira Patrol, the blockading of oil shipments to Rhodesia through Mozambique. Sold to Chile in 1982, she was "borrowed" back for the Falklands War, sailing to Curacao via the Panama Canal to pick up a UK crew, then proceeding south to support the 'Fearless' group. Following the war she was returned to Chile where she served as ALMIRANTE GORGE MONTT until decommissioning in 1997.

A Tide class fleet replenishment tanker, she was built by Sir James Laing & Sons, Sunderland, entering service in August 1955. The Tide class were the first Admiralty-designed purpose-built Fleet replenishment tankers intended for enduring front-line support. She was originally to have been named TIDERANGE but this was changed prior to entering service. Three ships were completed for the RFA with a further ship built for the Royal Australian Navy. Two further ships were laid down in the early 1960s to a modified design (see TIDEPOOL). The class had ice strengthened hulls to enable them to operate in Northern Waters. Replenishment equipment comprised five RAS rigs, three on the port side primarily so that they could fuel aircraft carriers and two on the starboard side along with the capability to refuel up to two ships over the stern. These ships carried Furnace Fuel Oil (FFO), Dieso, Aviation Spirit, both Avcat and Avgas, as well as a range of Lubricating oils and Fresh Water and limited dry stores. TIDESURGE was laid up at Portsmouth for disposal in May 1976 and arrived at Valencia for breaking up in June 1979.

RFA TIDESURGE (Image No: BW724505)

Ordered under the 1941 construction programme as the Minotaur class cruiser BELLEROPHON she was built by John Brown, Clydebank and launched on 25 October 1945, after which work was suspended. Work resumed in 1954, to a new design, and she was completed in March 1959. Her modern twin 6-inch MkXXVI turrets had a phenomenal rate of fire - 20 rounds per gun per minute, enabling them to deliver a greater weight of shell with their four guns than the earlier Town and Colony class had done with twelve. Initially she served in Home Waters and the Mediterranean. Following a refit in 1961 she served for a period in the Far East. In 1966, she hosted talks between Prime Ministers Harold Wilson (UK) and Ian Smith of Rhodesia. She entered reserve in 1966 following which, from 1968-72, she was converted at Devonport to a helicopter cruiser. Her after 6-inch and midship 3-inch turrets were removed and replaced with a flight deck and hangar to operate Anti-submarine Wessex and later Sea King helicopters. She paid off in 1978 and was placed on the disposal list in 1980. She was sold to Desguaces Varela and broken up in Spain in 1986.

HMS TIGER (Image No: BWP37)

A Group III 'T' class submarine built by HM Dockyard Portsmouth, she was completed in April 1945. She was one of seventeen such submarines ordered under the 1941 construction programme. Although later boats were to be of welded construction, TIRELESS was still riveted. In 1950 approval was given for five of the riveted 'T' class to undergo streamlined modernisation, in which programme TIRELESS was included, entering refit in 1951. She remained in service until August 1963 when she was put on the sale list. She was scrapped at Newport in 1968.

HMS TIRELESS (Image No: BW24748)

Another Group III 'T' class submarine built by Vickers Armstrong, Barrow, she was launched in May 1942 and completed in September the same year. The early Group I submarines were fitted with eight bow torpedo tubes and two external tubes amidships angled to fire forwards. Later Group II boats retained the ten torpedo tubes, but the midships pair were angled to face aft and a further tube fitted aft. The Group III boats were similar but welding allowed for greater diving depths and wartime austerity meant that some items, such as guardrails and a second anchor were deleted and much of the internal pipework was steel rather than copper. TRESPASSER served initially in the Mediterranean before transferring to the Indian Ocean. She survived the war and eventually arrived at J.J. King, Gateshead, for breaking up in September 1961.

HMS TRESPASSER (Image No: BW21021)

A 'T' class destroyer she was built by John Brown, Clydebank, completing in April 1943. Although outwardly similar to most other Emergency War Destroyers, she differed in being completed with a trial installation of two single, fixed, forward firing torpedo tubes angled outwards abaft her funnel rather than the standard quadruple mounting. During WWII she gained seven Battle Honours. Post-war she was placed in reserve at Portsmouth, where she remained until 1953 when she was brought forward to undergo conversion to a Type 16 frigate. Completing in 1954 she became part of the 2nd TS at Portsmouth. By December 1957 she was back in reserve, initially at Chatham and then, from 1960, at Rosyth. She was sold for scrap and arrived at Arnott Young, Dalmuir, in October 1965.

HMS TUMULT (Image No: BW20745)

A Hecla class destroyer depot ship, she was built by Scotts at Greenock and completed in February 1941. She served with the Home Fleet until 1944 and then transferred to the Pacific. In 1947 she was in reserve at Harwich and two years later refitted at Devonport. In 1950 she was reserve fleet depot ship at Malta and in 1952 Flagship of Flag Officer, Second-in-Command, Far East in Japanese waters during the Korean War. In 1954 she returned to Devonport and became Flagship of C-in-C Home Fleet. From 1957-58 she underwent a refit at Portsmouth and in 1961 became an accommodation ship, first at Portsmouth and then at Devonport. In 1968 she was allocated as maintenance ship for the reserve fleet at Devonport. In September 1972 she was broken up at Barrow.

HMS TYNE (Image No: BW18928)

HMS ULSTER, a Type 15 ASW Frigate, was originally built as an Emergency War class destroyer by Swan Hunter, Tyne and Wear. She was launched on 9 November 1942 and commissioned on 30 June the following year. Following duty in the English Channel, Mediterranean and Adriatic she was deployed as part of the British Pacific Fleet in 1945. She was damaged by a near miss by a Kamikaze and had to be towed to Leyte Gulf for repairs. She returned to the UK in October 1945 for full repairs at Chatham. Between 1953-55 she underwent conversion to a Type 15 frigate, following which she served with both the 8th and 2nd Frigate Squadrons. She was withdrawn from service in 1977 and broken up at T.W. Ward in 1980.

HMS ULSTER (Image No: BW712907)

Built by Vickers and completed in 1966. She was the first all British designed nuclear-powered submarine, substituting the US S5W nuclear plant, used in the earlier DREADNOUGHT, for a British designed system. In 1967 she completed a 28 day submerged transit from Singapore to the UK, at the time, a record for an RN submarine. She saw service in the Falklands War and underwent her third refit in 1989. By 1990 the class were becoming worn out and there were increasing concerns over reliability. In 1994 she was withdrawn from service and remains afloat at Devonport while a decision is made on how to dispose of her.

Britain's last battleship, she was built by John Brown and Co. Ltd. on Clydebank, being completed on 25 April 1946. She had a number of features incorporating lessons learned during WWII. A flared bow provided better sea keeping and she carried a plentiful array of AA guns. In 1947 she carried HM King George VI on a tour of South Africa. From 1948-54 she carried out fleet and training duties interspersed with various exercises. She became Flagship of the Home Fleet until 1954 when she was refitted and placed in reserve.The ship was towed from Portsmouth on 4 August bound for demolition on the Clyde - however, reluctant to depart, she ran aground off the Still & West pub near the harbour entrance. However, this only delayed the inevitable by a few hours and five days later she arrived at Faslane to begin breaking up.

HMS VANGUARD (Image No: BW10515)

An ocean going survey vessel VIDAL was built at Chatham Dockyard - the last surface vessel built at the Dockyard. She was also the first small ship designed to carry a helicopter. She was completed in March 1954 and operated in Home Waters before moving on to the West Indies, returning to Chatham in the December. The next eleven years were spent surveying in Home and West Indies waters with regular refits at Chatham. From 1966 her surveying duties were in the Far East until 1970 when she paid off for disposal. She was broken up at Bruges in 1976.

A W-class destroyer she was built Fairfield Shipbuilding and Engineering Company, Govan as part of the 9th Emergency Flotilla. She was launched on 30 June 1943 and completed in 1944. She saw war service in the Atlantic, Indian and Pacific Oceans. Post war she operated as a training ship until being taken in hand for conversion under the Type 15 programme in 1951. The work was undertaken by Scott's Shipbuilding Company, Greenock, completing in 1953. As seen here all superstructure to deck level was removed and replaced with a lower structure extending aft to the quarterdeck. The principal anti-submarine armament was a pair of Mark 10 Limbo A/S mortars. Following service with the 5th FS in the Mediterranean she was converted to a Navigation Training ship in 1957, replacing STARLING. From 1966-67 she undertook trials of stabilisers and satellite communications equipment. In 1970 she left Portsmouth for de-equipping at Rosyth arriving at Inverkeithing a year later to be broken up by Thomas Ward.

A Fairmile B Motor Launch she was built by the Anglo-American Nile Tourist Yard at Cairo and completed in June 1944 as ML 840. Post war she was found suitable for further service and was redesignated ML 2840 in 1950 and would serve as a minesweeping launch. Whilst in refit at Portsmouth, in 1954, it was decided to allocate the vessel to the Fishery Protection Flotilla to replace an elderly MFV. In 1955 she was commissioned for fishery protection duties and in November that year was renamed WATCHFUL. She remained in that role until replaced by BROOMLEY in 1959. WATCHFUL was placed on the disposal list in 1962.

Built by Furness Shipbuilding Company, Haverton Hill, she was laid down as the EMPIRE FLODDEN for the Ministry of War Transport, but launched as RFA WAVE BARON in June 1946. One of twenty such ships acquired by the Admiralty, these steam-powered vessels were the fore runner of the modern day fleet tanker. WAVE BARON served during the Korean War and from 1957 - 1960 supported Operation Grapple- the British H-bomb tests at Christmas Island in the Pacific Ocean. She arrived at Devonport for the final time on 28 October 1969 and in 1972 was placed on the disposal list and in April that same year arrived at Bilbao, Spain, for breaking up by Revalorizacion de Materials SA.

A Tribal class general purpose frigate built by Alex Stephen & Sons, Govan, she was completed in 1964. A single shaft design, ZULU was unique among the Tribals in that she was fitted with two quadruple Seacat launchers either side of the mast from build. The remainder of the class were fitted initially with two single 40mm Bofors. They were fitted with Seacat in the 1970s using systems removed from the Battle class and County class refits. ZULU joined 9th FS east of Suez until August 1965 when she returned to the UK. In 1979 she joined the Standby Squadron at Chatham, but was recommissioned in 1982 during the Falklands War to cover for ships lost and damaged. She paid off in 1984 and was transferred to Indonesia, being renamed MARTHA KHRYSTINA TIYAHADU.